Book 1
Robotics
By Kenneth Fraser

&

Book 2
Open Source
By Solis Tech

Book 1
Robotics
By **Kenneth Fraser**

The Beginner's Guide to Robotic Building, Technology, Mechanics, and Processes!

Table of Contents

Introduction

I want to thank you and congratulate you for purchasing the book, *"Robotics: The Beginner's Guide to Robotic Building"*.

This book contains proven steps and strategies on how to build your own robot that will perform certain functions as you want it to do.

For most people, a robot is a machine that could mimic a human such as R2D2 and C3PO in Star Wars. But these types of robots are still in the figments of our imaginations. We are still far from giving robots high level of artificial intelligence to easily adapt and interact to its environment. There is however pioneering works on artificial intelligence that hopes to create humanoid robots.

The type of robots that exist and working today are robots that are programmed to do things that are too dangerous for humans, too repetitive, or just plain messy. These robots are often found in wide range of industries and places such as oil refineries, hospitals, laboratories, factories, and even in the Outer Space. There are about more than a million robots are working in different fields today.

There are types of robots that bring joy to kids such as the popular AIBO ERS-220 that is a bestseller toy during Christmas. While some robots perform great feats by discovering new places and gathering important data in the name of science, specialized robots such as the Mars Rover Sojourner and the underwater robot Caribou are sent to places that average humans cannot go.

Robots are exciting machines to play with, but they are more exciting to build. For hobbyists, building their own robots that capable of doing whatever they program these machines to do gives them pure delight.

This book introduces you to the science of robotics – its basic elements and fundamental concepts. And at the course of your reading, you will learn all the essential aspects you need to build your own robot.

Thanks again for purchasing this book, I hope you enjoy it!

Chapter 1 – What is a Robot?

It is interesting to know that even with all the hype about robots and with all the milestones in robotics, there is still not standard definition for a robot. There are, however, some basic characteristics that a robot should have and this could help you determine if a certain object is a robot or not. It will also guide you in deciding what features you need to build into a machine before you can say that it is a robot.

Four Basic Characteristics of a Robot

A robot has four basic characteristics: sensing, movement, intelligence, and energy.

Sensing

Basically, a robot must be capable of sensing its environment much similar to the way humans sense its surroundings. Robots could either sense through light sensors that mimic the functions of the eyes, or be equipped with chemical sensors that function like the nose, sonar sensors like the nose, touch sensors like the skin, and taste sensors like the tongue. These sensors will help the robot to become aware and understand its environment.

Movement

A robot should have the ability to move around through walking on legs, rolling on wheels, or through propellers. It's either the entire robot is able to move or just some parts of it such as head, arms, or just legs.

Intelligence

A robot should be equipped with artificial intelligence or AI. This is usually done through computer programing. Hence, you need a background in programming to provide your robot with the needed intelligence. You need to program the robot's intelligence so that it will know what to sense and how to move.

Energy

A robot should have a way to power itself. The energy source could be electrical, chemical (battery), or solar. The method by which your robot energizes itself depends on what your robot is required to do.

Working Definition of a Robot

For the purpose of discussion and for reference, we define robot as a machine that contains control systems, sensors, manipulators, software and power supplies that works together to do certain tasks.

Building a robot requires understanding of the fundamental principles of mechanical engineering, mathematics, physics, and computer programming. In special cases, it also requires specific knowledge on chemistry, biology, and medicine. In studying robotics, you need to be actively engaged with wide range of disciplines to build robots that could solve certain problems.

A Brief History of Robotics

The word "robot" was first used in a play entitled R.U.R (Rossum's Universal Robots) written in 1921 by Czech writer Karl Capek. This play is about machines that are built to work on a factory and eventually revolted against their human masters. Robots are the Czech word for slave.

Meanwhile, the word robotics also first appeared in a work of fiction. Russian-born American fictionist Isaac Asimov used it in his short story "Runabout" (1942). Compared to Capek, Asimov had a more positive opinion of the role of robots in the society. In general, he described robots as useful machines that serve humans and perceived them as a "better, cleaner race. He also proposed the three Laws of Robotics:

First Law of Robotics

A robot may not injure a human or, through inaction, allow a human to come to harm.

Second Law of Robotics

A robot must obey the orders given by humans except if such orders would violate the First Law.

Third Law of Robotics

A robot may protect itself as long as such protection do not violate with the First Law or Second Law of Robotics.

Early Models of Robots

Among the earliest cases of a mechanical system designed to perform a regular task was recorded around 3000 BCE. Egyptian water clocks are added with human statuettes to hit the hour bells and signal the passing of time. In 400 BCE,

Archytus of Taremtum, who was known as the inventor of pulley and screw, created a pigeon made of wood that is capable of flying. Meanwhile, hydraulically-powered figurines that could speak prophecies were common during the Greek domination of Egypt during the second century BCE.

In the first century C.E., Petronius Arbiter built a doll that is capable of moving like a human being. In 1557, Giovanni Torriani built a wooden robot, which could fetch the Emperor's bread every day from the store. By 1700s, robotic inventions became common with numerous impractical yet ingenious machines such as steam-powered automata crafted in Canada as well as the popular talking doll by Thomas Edison. Even though these creations may have inspired the design and functions for the modern robot, the progress during the 20th century in the field of robotics exceeded previous advancements many times over.

The First Modern Robots

The robots that we are familiar with were built by George C. Devol in the 1950s. The inventor from Kentucky designed and patented a reprogrammable manipulator that he dubbed as "Unimate" derived from "Universal Automation." For years, he tried commercializing his product, but failed. But in 1960s, the entrepreneur-engineer Joseph Englberger bought the patent from Devol and modified it into an industrial robot. He established his company, Unimation, for production and marketing of these products. He was successful in this venture, and in fact, Englberger is regarded today as the Father of Robotics.

Robotics also progressed within the academic institutions. Alan Turing, pioneering computer scientist, mathematician, logician, and cryptologist, published his book "Computing Machiner and Intelligence" where he proposed a test to determine if a machine has the capacity to think for itself. This test is known as the Turing Test.

In 1958, Charles Rosen of the Stanford Research Institute created a research team to work in the development or a robot known as "Shakey" that was more advanced compared to Devol's Unimate. Shakey can move around through the room, sense light through his "eyes" move around strange environment, and to a particular degree, and react to what is happening to his surroundings. He was called Shakey because of his clattering and rickety motions.

In 1966 at Massachusetts Institute of Technology (MIT), Joseph Weizenbaum created an artificial program named ELIZA, which functions as a computer psychologist that manipulates its user's statements to formulate questions.

In 1967, Richard Greenblatt developed MacHack, a program that is capable of playing chess, as a response to a critical article written by Hubert Dreyfuss where he boasted that no computer program can beat him in chess. When the program is finished, Dreyfuss was invited to play and was defeated. This program was the foundation of future chess programs that eventually developed into Big Blue, the program that defeated Grand Master Gary Kasparov in 1997.

The interest in robotics is one of the major catalysts in the development of computers. In 1964, the IBM 360 becomes the first computer to be produced massively.

Robots are also crucial in pioneering space explorations. In 1969, the United States successfully used the latest technology in robotics and computing for Neil Armstrong's landing on the moon. Robots also helped in the expansion of scientific knowledge. In 1994, Carnegie Universities crafted Dante II, an eight-legged walking robot that successfully descends into the crater of Mt Spur to gather samples of volcanic gas.

Commercial companies also leveraged on the mass appeal of robots. In 1999, Sony released its original version of AIBO, a robotic dog that can entertain, learn, and communicate with its owner. Advanced versions have followed in the succeeding years, with the final model, the ERS-7M3, released in 2005.

Honda also released its ASIMO robot, an advanced humanoid robot in 2000. In 2004, Epsom was hailed as the world's smallest robot (7 cm high and weighs only 10 g.) The robotic helicopter is designed to fly and capture videos during natural disasters.

After being released in 2002, a robotic vacuum cleaner known as the Roomba became a huge hit. It sold more than 2.5 million units, which shows that there's really a huge demand for domestic robot technology.

Hundreds of films feature robots such as The Day the Earth Stood Still (1951), Arthur C. Clark's 2001: A Space Odyssey (1968), Star Wars (1977), Blade Runner (1982), Terminator (1984), Nemesis (1992), I, Robot (2004), Transformers (2007), and many more. The popularity of robotic films shows that people are inspired and delighted by the idea of machines that can independently move and think for itself.

If you are ready to build your own robot, continue to the next Chapter to help you get started.

Chapter 2 – Get Started

The first step in building your own robot is to determine what it should do, that is, your purpose of why you are building the robot. Robots can be used in different situations and are mainly designed to assist humans. It will help you a lot to learn first the different purposes and uses of robots.

Basically, robots are divided into two main groups: industrial and domestic robots.

Industrial Robots

Industrial robots are used in factories to manufacture products with precisions such as computers, cars, cellphones, medicine, and even food. Robots increased the productivity in different workplaces, which resulted to booming industries. Each type of industrial robot has its specific form that corresponds to its function. For instance, robotic arms are often used in car assembly lines to spray paint or weld frames. Robotic arms are among the most common robots today. Recently, agricultural robots have been introduced mainly to perform farm tasks such as cutting weeds and harvesting crops.

Domestic Robots

Domestic robots are mainly used in the home to perform household chores. They usually perform repetitive tasks every day such as vacuuming floors, mowing the lawn, vacuuming floors, and other chores that people usually don't have time to do. For example, there are vacuum robots that can clean the floors. They are equipped with motion sensors so they will not run into any object. You just need to push the switch on and it will do its job. It could pick up dust and pet hairs and could be used for hours.

There are also mower robots that could mow lawns. They are equipped with sensors to detect grass edges. Domestic robots are also used for entertainment such as Robosapien, AIBO, and iDog.

Choosing a Robotic Platform

The next step in building your own robot is to decide on the type of robot you want to build. A usual robot design usually begins with "inspiration" of what the robot will do and what it will look like.

The types of robots that you can build are endless. As long as you can envision something that a robot can do, you can work your way to achieve it. But for beginners, you can start with the following types: land robots, aerial robots, aquatic robots, stationary robots, and hybrid robots.

Land Robots

Land-based robots, particularly those added with wheels are among the most common mobile robots built by beginners, because they often require minimal investment while providing the opportunity to learn more about robotics. Meanwhile, the most advanced type of robot is the humanoid robot, which is akin to humans. Humanoids require several degrees of freedom and synchronization of different motors and use several sensors.

Wheeled Robots

Wheels are among the most common method of adding mobility to a robot and are used to mobilize many different sizes of robots and robotic platforms. Wheels could be about any size, and there's no limit in the number of wheels that you can add. More often than not, robots that are equipped with three wheels are using two wheels and a caster at one end. More advanced robots with two wheels are using gyroscopic stabilizing technology.

Meanwhile, robots that are added with four to six wheels usually use several drive motors that decreases the risk of slippage. Also, mecanum wheels or omni-directional wheels can provide the robot considerable benefits in mobility. Most beginners in robotic building are mistaken in thinking that inexpensive DC motors can mobilize robots that are medium in size. As you will learn later, there are more factors that you need to consider before you can add mobility to your robot.

Advantages

Wheeled robots are ideal for beginners as they are often more affordable to build. They have simple design and construction, and there are unlimited options. In addition, robots with six wheels or more could rival the mobility of a track system.

Disadvantages

Wheeled robots usually have small contact area, because only a small portion of the wheel is touching the ground. This results to lower traction that may cause slippage.

Tracked Robots

Tracks are used in tanks for mobility. Even though tracks, also known as treads, don't provide the added torque, they can decrease slippage and can equally distribute the robot's weight. This makes the robot easier to mobilize in loose ground such as gravel and sand. In addition, flexible track systems could easily navigate through a bumpy surface. Most hobbyists also believe that tank tracks are quite cool compared to wheels.

Advantages

Steady contact with the ground avoids slippage, which is prevalent with wheels. The track system also distributes weight evenly, which helps the robot in navigating different surfaces. Tracks can also be used to extensively enhance the ground clearance of the robot without adding a bigger drive wheel.

Disadvantages

The main disadvantage of using a track system for robots is that in turning, there's the tendency to cause damage to the surface that also causes damage to the tracks. In addition, robots are often built around the tracks, and there's a limit in the availability of the tracks. Drive sprocket can also considerably restrict the number of motors that you can use.

Legged Robots

More and more robots are using legs for movement. Legs are usually ideal to use for robots that should navigate on uneven ground. Many prototype robots are built with six legs that allow the robot for static balance. Robots with fewer legs are more difficult to balance as it requires dynamic stability. Once the robot ceases moving in the middle of the stride, it could fall over. Even though there were robots with one leg moving by hopping, bipeds, quadrupeds, and hexapods are the most common forms.

Advantages

The leg motion is the most natural among the platforms, and it can easily overcome big obstacles and move through rough surface.

Disadvantages

Most beginners are discouraged in building their first robot that moves using legs, as it requires high level of electronic, mechanical and coding skills. You also need to find a small battery that can provide the required power, so legged robots are usually expensive to build.

Aerial Robots

Humans have long been inspired by the idea of flight, and this transcends into the field of robotics. The idea of Autonomous Unmanned Aerial Vehicle (AUAV) has gained popularity over the years, and many enthusiasts have developed numerous prototypes. However, the benefits of crafting aerial robots have yet to prevail over the disadvantages. In building aerial robots, many hobbyists are still using commercial remote controllers. Professional aircrafts such as the Predator commissioned by the US military were partially autonomous though recently, updated versions of the Predator have completed aerial missions with only minimum human intervention.

Advantages

Aerial robots are great for surveillance, and remote controlled aircraft has been developed through the years, so there is a diverse community for mechanics where you can find support and know-how in building your own aerial robots.

Disadvantages

There is still limited community when it comes to autonomous control, as most of the knowledge on this field is protected by the US military. Meanwhile, this robot type is expensive as the whole robot could be broken if you miscalculate the steps and lead the robot into a crash.

Aquatic Robots

Recently, more and more hobbyists, communities, and companies are building unnamed aquatic vehicles. There are still many hindrances to overcome in order to make aquatic robots more enticing for the wider communities in robotics. But it is interesting to take note that there are companies today who are manufacturing robots that can clean pools. Aquatic robots can use thrusters, ballast, wings, tails, and fins to move under water.

Advantages

A massive part of the ocean is still unexplored so there's a lot to discover if you choose to build aquatic robots that could help in discovering the underwater world. The robot design is also guaranteed to be unique, and it could be tested in a pool.

Disadvantages

Aquatic robots are often very expensive to build, and there is the risk that the robot could be lost while deep in the ocean. You should also take note that most electronic parts don't pair well with water, especially salty water. You also need to consider the water pressure as going beyond deep sea needs considerable investment and research. There is also very limited robotic community that can provide support, and also limited wireless communication options.

Hybrid Robots

Your concept for the robot may not easily fall into any of the categories mentioned above or could be composed of various functional components. Take note that this book is written to guide you in building mobile robots and not those with fixed designs. In building a hybrid design, it is best to use a modular design where each functional component could be taken off and tested as a separate part.

Advantages

Hybrid robots are designed and built according to your preferences and needs. These robots could be used for various tasks and can be composed of modules. Hybrid robots could lead to versatility and increased functionality.

Disadvantages

Hybrid robots are often complicated to build and expensive. Parts need to be customized to fit the design.

Grippers and Arms

Even though grippers and arms don't fall under the category of mobile robots, robotics basically began with end-effectors and arms. Grippers and arms are the most ideal way for a robot to interact with the environment it is dealing with. Basic robotic arms could have just two to three motions; while more advanced arms could have more than a dozen movements.

Advantages

Most robotic arms and grippers have simple designs, and it is easy to make a three to four degree of freedom robotic arm with a turning base and two joints.

Disadvantages

Robotic arms are stationary unless you fix them on a mobile platform. The cost of building arms or grippers depends on the lifting capacity you need.

In the next chapter, you will learn how to choose the right actuators or motors for your robot.

Chapter 3 – Understanding Actuators

After learning general information about robots and robotics in the first two chapters, it is now time to choose the right actuators to mobilize your robot.

What Are Actuators?

Actuators are devices that transform energy into physical motion. In robotics, this energy is usually electrical energy. Most actuators today produce either linear or rotational motion. For example, a DC motor is a type of actuator.

Selecting the right actuator for your robot requires learning the available actuators, and some fundamental knowledge of physics and mathematics.

Rotational Actuators

Rotational actuators convert electrical energy into rotating motion. There are two primary mechanical parameters that distinguish each actuator: (a) the rotational speed that is often measured in revolutions per minute or rpm and (b) torque or the force that the devices can produce at a given distance often expressed in Oz•in or N•m.

AC Motor

Alternating Current (AC) is rarely used in robots because most of them are powered through Direct Current (DC) in form of cells or batteries. In addition, electronic parts use DC, so it is easier to use the same type of power supply for the actuators. AC motors are primary used in industrial settings where high torque is necessary or where the motors are connected to a wall outlet.

DC Motor

DC motors are often cylindrical in shape but they also come in different shapes and sizes. They also have output shafts that rotate at high speed often between 5000 and 10000 rpm. Even though DC motors rotate very fast, most have low torque. To decrease the speed and add torque, a gear could be added. To install a motor into a robot, you must fix the body of the motor to the robot's frame. Hence, motors usually have mounting holes that are basically located on the motor's face so that they can be easily installed. DC motors could either rotate in counter clockwise or clockwise. The angular movement of the turning shaft could be measured using potentiometers and encoders.

Geared DC Motor

A DC Motor could be added with a gearbox to reduce the motor's speed and enhance its torque. For instance, if a DC motor rotates at 5000 rpm and produces a 0.0005 N•m of torque, adding a 123:1 ("one hundred and twenty three to one") gear would reduce the speed by a factor of 123 (resulting to 5000 rpm / 123 = 40 rpm) and increase the torque by a factor of 123 (0.0005 x 123 = 0.0615 N•m). The most common types of gears are planetary, spur, and worm. Similar to a DC motor, a geared DC motor can also rotate in either clockwise or counter clockwise. You can add an encoder to the shaft if you want to know the number of rotations of the motor.

Hobby Servo Motors

Hobby Servo Motors, also known as R/C Servo Motors are actuators that rotate to a certain angular position, and were traditionally used in more expensive remote controlled machines for controlling or steering flight surfaces. Today, they are used in different applications so their prices have been reduced considerably, and the variety has also increased. Most servo motors can only rotate about 180 degrees. A hobby servo motor is composed of a DC motor, electronics, gears, and a potentiometer that measures the angle. The latter works with the electronics to mobilize the motor and stop the output shaft at a certain angle. In general, these servos have three wires, voltage in, control pulse, and ground. A robot servo is a recently developed servo that provides both position feedback and continuous rotation. Servos could rotate clockwise or counterclockwise.

Stepper Motors

As the name implies, stepper motors rotates following certain steps or degrees. The number of degrees the shaft rotates with every step could vary depending on various factors. Majority of stepper motors don't include gears, so similar to a DC motor, the torque is quote low. Fixing gears to a stepper motor has similar effect as installing gears to a DC motor.

Linear Actuators

Linear actuators produce linear movements. They have three primary distinctive mechanical properties: (a) the force measured in kg or lbs (b) speed measured in m/s or inch/s and (c) the maximum and minimum distance that the rod could move also known as the stroke measured in inches or mm.

Linear DC Actuator

A linear DC actuator is usually composed of a DC motor attached to a lead screw, which also turns as the motor moves. The lead screw has a traveler that is forced either away or towards the motor, basically transforming the rotating motion to a linear movement. Some DC linear actuators integrate a linear potentiometer that adds a linear position feedback.

Solenoids

Solenoids are comprised of a coil wound surrounding the mobile core. Once the coil is energized, the core is forced away from the magnetic field and creates a motion in one direction. Several coils or some mechanical arrangements will be needed to provide movements in different directions. A solenoid stroke is often very small but they are often very fast. The strength primarily depends on the size of the coil and the electrical power passing through it.

Hydraulic and Pneumatic Actuators

Hydraulic and pneumatic actuators use liquid or air respectively to create a linear movement. These actuators could have lengthy strokes, high speed and high force. To use these actuators, you need to use a fluid or air compressor that makes them harder to use compared to basic electrical actuators. These are often used in industrial applications because of their large size and high force speed.

Muscle Wire

Muscle wire is a specialized wire, which contracts when electricity passes through it. When electricity is gone and once the wire cools down, it will go back to its original length. This type of actuator is not fast, strong, or creates a long stroke. Nonetheless, it is one of the most convenient actuators to use if you need to work with smaller parts.

How to Choose the Proper Actuator for Your Robot

To guide you in choosing the actuator for certain tasks, consider answering the following questions to help you.

Take note that new innovations and technologies are always being released regularly, so nothing is permanent. Also remember that one actuator could perform various tasks in various contexts.

1. Do you need to mobilize a wheeled robot?

Drive motors should carry the weight of the whole robot and will most likely need a gear down. Majority of the robots utilize "skid steering" while trucks or cars utilize rack and pinion steering. If you prefer the skid steering, geared DC motors are recommended to use for robots with tracks or wheels. Geared motors provide constant rotation, and could have discretionary position feedback through optical encoders. Because the rotation needed is limited to a certain angle, you can choose a hobby servo motor for stirring.

2. Is there a limit on the range of motion?

If the range is restricted to 180 degrees and the needed torque is not a critical factor, a hobby servo motor is recommended. Servo motors are available in various torques and sizes and comes with angular position feedback. Majority of these motors use potentiometer, while some specialized ones use optical encoders. R/C servos are now popularly used to build small walking robots.

3. Do you need a motor to lift or turn heavy loads?

Raising a weight needs considerably more power compare to moving a weight on a flat surface. Torque should be prioritized than the speed, and it is ideal to use a gearbox with a powerful DC motor or a linear DC actuator with a high gear ratio. You can use an actuator system that could prevent the mass from falling if there is a disruption in the power source. This includes clamps or worm gears.

4. Do you need the angle to be precise?

Stepper motors that are paired with a motor controller cold provide a very precise angular motion. They are more ideal to use compared to servo motors because they provide constant rotation. But there are also high-end digital servo motors that use optical encoders and can provide high precision.

5. Do you need to achieve movements in a straight line?

Linear actuators are ideal for moving parts and placing them in a straight line. They are available in different configurations and sizes. For fast movements, you must consider solenoids or pneumatics, for high torques, you can use linear DC actuators or hydraulics, and if the movement requires minimum torque, you can use muscle wire.

Chapter 4 - Microcontrollers and Motor Controllers

Microcontrollers are considered as the "brain" of the robot because it is responsible for all decision making, computations, and communications. These are devices with the capacity to execute a program (a series of instructions).

To interact with the external world, a microcontroller has a sequence of electrical signal connections (known as pins), which could be switched on or off using programming functions. These pins are also used in reading electronic signals that are released by sensors or other devices and determine if they are low or high.

Majority of microcontrollers today could measure analogue voltage signals, or signals that could have a full range of values rather than just two specified states by using analog to digital converter or ADC. Through the use of ADC, a microcontroller could assign a numerical value to the analog voltage that is neither low nor high.

What Could Microcontrollers Do?

Numerous complicated actions could be achieved by setting the pins low and high creatively. Nonetheless, building complicated algorithms such as smart movements and data processing or complicated programs are not yet on the range of microcontrollers because of its natural speed and resource limitations.

For example, to light a blinker, you can program a repeating sequence in which the microcontrollers could turn a pin high, wait for several seconds, turn it low, wait for several seconds and goes back to the first sequence. A light that is connected to the pin will then blink open-endedly.

Similarly, microcontrollers could be used to take control of other electronic devices including actuators when they are installed to motor controllers, Bluetooth or WiFi interfaces, storage devices, and many more. Because of its versatility, microcontrollers could be found in common everyday products. Basically, every home electrical device or home appliance utilizes at least one microcontroller.

Not similar to microprocessors found in Central Processing Units in personal computers, microcontrollers don't need peripherals such as external storage devices or external RAM to operate. Hence, even if the microcontrollers are less powerful compared to microprocessors, building circuits and products based on microcontrollers is an easier task and a lot more affordable, because minimal hardware parts are needed. Remember, microcontrollers can output minimum amount of electrical power through pins. Hence, a generic microcontroller cannot power solenoids, power electrical motors, large lights, or other direct loads. Doing this could cause physical damage to the controller.

Programming Microcontrollers

There's no need to shy away from programming microcontrollers. Not similar in the past where making a blinker took comprehensive knowledge of microcontroller and at least a dozen line of code, programming microcontrollers is fairly easy today. You can use the simplified Integrated Development Environments (IDE), which uses modern languages, full line archives that could cover all of the most common actions, and several handy samples to help you get started. You can learn more about programming your robot in Chapter 6.

How to Choose the Proper Microcontroller for Your Robot

You will need a microcontroller for any robotic building project unless you're into BEAM robotics or you want to control your robot through an R/C system or a tether. For starters, selecting the right microcontroller could seem like a difficult job, particularly considering the product range, specifications, and applications. There are various microcontrollers available today such as BasicATOM, POB Technology, Pololu, Arduino, BasicX, and Parallax.

The following questions could guide you in choosing the right microcontroller:

1. Which microcontroller is widely used for your type of robotic project?

Building robots is not a popularity contest, but the fact that a microcontroller has a large supporting community or has been used in the same project can make the design phase easily. With this, you can benefit from other experience and hobbyists. It is common for hobbyists to share codes, pictures, instructions, and videos even lessons learned.

2. Do you need specific accessories for a certain microcontroller?

If your robot has special needs or there is a certain accessory or component that is important for your design, selecting a compatible microcontroller is clearly essential. Even though most accessories and sensors could be directly interfaced with most microcontrollers, some accessories are designed to interface with a particular microcontroller.

3. Do you need special features for your robot?

A microcontroller should be able to perform all the special actions needed for your robot to function well. Some features are common to all microcontrollers such as being able to execute basic mathematical operations, having digital inputs and outputs, and making decisions. Others may need certain hardware such as PWM, ADC, and communication protocol support. You must also consider pin counts, memory and speed requirements

Motor Controllers

Motor controllers are electronic devices that serve an intermediary device between a microcontroller, the motors, and the power supply.

Even though the microcontroller decides the direction and the speed of the motors, it doesn't have enough power to directly drive them. Meanwhile, the motor controller can supply the current at the needed voltage but doesn't have the capacity to decide how fast the motor must turn.

Hence, the microcontroller and the motor controller must work together to make the motors move accordingly. The microcontroller can provide instructions to the motor controller on how to power up the motors through a standard and basic communication method such as PWM and UART. In addition, some motor controllers could be manually regulated using an analog voltage often created through a potentiometer.

The size and weight of a motor controller may greatly vary from a device that is smaller than the tip of a pencil to a huge controller that could weight several kilos. The size and weight often has a minimum effect on the robot, unless you want to build unnamed aerial or aquatic robots.

Types of Motor Controllers

Because there are several types of actuators (as we have discussed in Chapter 3), there are also several types of motor controllers: brushed DC motor controllers, brushless DC motor controllers, servo motor controllers, and stepper motor controllers.

How to Choose a Motor Controller

You can only choose a motor controller after you have decided on what type of actuator you want to use. In addition, the current that a motor draws depends on the torque it could provide. A small DC motor will not use much current, but cannot also release much torque, while a bigger motor could release higher torque but will need increased current.

Chapter 5 - Controlling Your Robot and Use of Sensors

Based on our definition of a robot, it should gather data about its surroundings, make smart decisions and then execute actions based on calculations. This also includes the option for the robot to become semi-autonomous (with aspect that are controlled by humans and other aspects that it can do on its own).

One good example of this is a complex aquatic robot. A human controls the basic motions of the robot while an installed processor measures and reacts to the underwater currents to keep the robot in one position while still preventing a drift. A camera installed in the robot would send videos back to the human while the sensors could track the water pressure, temperature, and more. Once the communication line falters between the robot and the human, an autonomous program could take over to instruct the robot to reach for the surface.

In controlling your robot, you need to figure out the level of autonomy. You need to choose if you want the robot to be tethered, wireless, or autonomous.

Tethered

Direct Wired Control

The simplest way to control a vehicle is by using a handheld controller that is physically connected to a vehicle using a tether or a cable. Knobs, switches, joysticks, buttons, and levers on the controller will allow you to control the robot without the need to add sophisticated electronics. In this setting, the power source and motors could be directly connected with a switch to control the rotation. These machines often have no artificial intelligence and are regarded as remote controlled devices than robots.

Wired Computer Control

Another method is to integrate a microcontroller into the machine but still using a tether. Attaching the microcontroller to your computer's ports will allow you to control the actions using the keyboard, a joystick, a keypad, or other device. Adding a microcontroller to your robot project may also require programming how the robot will respond to the input.

Ethernet

Another way to use computer control is to use an Ethernet interface. A robot that is directly connected to a router can also be used for mobile robots. Building a robot, which can communicate through the internet could be sophisticated, and usually a wireless internet connection is more recommended.

Wireless

Infrared

You can ditch away cables and wires if you use infrared transmitters and receivers. This is often a great achievement for beginners. Infrared control needs "line of sight" to function. The receiver should have the ability to see the transmitter to receive the data. Infrared remote controls can be used to send commands to infrared receivers that are paired with microcontrollers that interpret these signals and control the actions of the robot.

Radio Frequency

Remote control units often use microcontrollers in the receiver and transmitter for data transmission through radio frequency. The receiver box usually has a printed circuit board (PCB) that includes a small servo motor controller and a receiving unit. RF communication needs a transmitter matched with a receiver or a transceiver. RF doesn't need clear line of sight and could also provide considerable distance. Basic RF devices could allow for data transfer between devices between long distances, and there's no limit to the range for more RF devices.

Bluetooth

Bluetooth is a type of Radio Frequency and follows certain protocols for sending and receiving data. Standard Bluetooth range is usually restricted to about 10 meters although it has the advantage of controlling the robot though Bluetooth-enabled devices including laptops, smartphones, and PDAs. Similar to RF, Bluetooth provides two-way communication.

WiFi

Recent development in wireless technology enables you to control a robot through the Internet. To build a WiFi robot, you must have a wireless router that is connected to the internet and a WiFi device on the robot. You can also use a device, which is enabled with TCP/IP with a wireless router.

Autonomous

High-level robots are autonomous. With recent developments, you can now use the microcontroller in its full potential and program it to respond to input from the sensors. Autonomous control may come in different types: restricted sensor feedback, pre-programmed with no feedback from the environment, and complex sensor feedback. Genuine "autonomous" control includes different sensors and code to allow the robot to figure out by itself the smartest action to be taken in any situation.

The most sophisticated methods of control presently used on autonomous robots are auditory and visual commands. For auditory control, a robot will react to the sound of the human's voice for instructions such as "get the ball" or "turn left." For visual command, a robot may look to an object to decide on what to do. Instructing a robot to turn to the right by showing a drawing of an arrow that is pointing to the right requires complicated programming. Even though these things are no longer impossible, they need a sophisticated level programming and usually hundreds of hours.

Not similar to humans, robots are not restricted to just sound, sight, smell, touch, and taste. Robots use different electromechanical sensors to understand and discover their surroundings. Mimicking a natural organism's senses is presently a great challenge, so developers and robotic builders are using alternatives to these natural senses.

Chapter 6 - Assembling and Programming a Robot

After learning all about the fundamental blocks in building a robot, the next stage is the designing and building of the frame that will keep all the components together and will provide your robot a definite look and shape.

Constructing the Frame

There's no fix method in creating a frame, because there is often a trade-off to be constructed. You may prefer to use a lightweight frame but you may need to use costly materials. You may like a strong or big chassis but you may realize it is expensive, hard, or heavy to produce. The frame could be complicated and may take some time to design and build.

Materials

There are different materials that you can use in creating a frame for your robot. As you try different materials to construct not only robots but other types of machines, you will also understand the advantages and the disadvantages as to which material is the most suitable for a specific project. The roster of suggested building materials below comprises only the more common one, and when you have tried several of these materials, you can start experimenting or blending some together.

Basic Construction Materials

Some of the most basic construction materials could be used to build good-quality frames. The cheapest materials is the cardboard that you can usually find for free and could easily be bent, cut, layered, or bent. You can construct a reinforced cardboard box that looks a lot nicer and is more proportional when it comes to the size of your robot. You can then paint it with glue or epoxy to make it stronger then add extra layer of paint.

Structural Flat Materials

For a more durable frame, you can use a standard structural material such as a sheet of plastic, metal, or wood. You just need to puncture some holes to connect the electronic components. A stronger piece of wood has a tendency to be heavy and thick, while a thin sheet of metal could be too flexible. You can attach components to both sides and the wood will still remain solid and intact.

If you're at the stage where you are ready to have an outsourced frame, the best option is to acquire the part precision cut through a water or laser jet. Hiring a third-party to produce a custom part is recommended only if you are completely sure of the dimensions, because the mistakes could be expensive. Companies that offer computer controlled cutting services may also provide different other services such as painting and bending.

3D Printing

Building a frame constructed from 3D printed panels is not always the most structurally sound option, primarily because it is built up in several layers. However, this process could produce complex and detailed shapes that could be impossible to build using other methods. One 3D printed component may contain all the important mounting points for all mechanical or electrical parts without compromising the robot's weight. In the past decade, the cost of 3D printing is quite expensive, but as it becomes popular, the price of producing the components is also expected to go down.

Assembling the Parts Together

With the available options for materials and methods, you can now start assembling the parts together. You can follow the steps below to build a simple, aesthetic, and structurally reliable robot frame.

1. Decide on the material you want to use.

2. Gather all the parts that your robot will need, both mechanical and electrical and measure them. In case you don't have all the components ready, you can refer to the dimensions that are often supplied by the manufacturers.

3. Think of and draw various designs for your frame. It's fine not to provide details.

4. Once you find the suitable design, be certain that the structure is reliable and all the parts would be supported in the frame.

5. Sketch every component of the robot on cardboard or paper at true scale. You can also draw the parts in the CAD software and print them.

6. Test the design in CAD and in actual setting using your paper prototype by test fitting every component and connection.

7. Measure the dimensions again and when you are completely certain that your design is right, begin cutting the frame into the material. Take note to measure two times and only cut once.

8. Test fit every part before assembling the frame if in case you need some changes.

9. Construct the frame using appropriate assembling materials such as glue, nails, screw, duct tape, or any appropriate binding tools that you prefer.

10. Fit all the parts into the frame and there you go, you have just built your robot!

Constructing the Robot Parts

The last step discussed above should be described further. In the past chapters, you have already chosen the electrical parts including the actuators, microcontroller, and motor controller. The next step is to construct them so they will work together.

In the following section, we'll use standard cable colors and terminal names that encompass common parts. You must rely on manuals and datasheets when you are working on your specific parts.

Attaching Motor Controllers to Motors

A geared DC motor or a linear DC actuator usually has two wires: black and red. Attach the black wire to the M- terminal on the DC motor controller and the red wire to the M+ terminal. Connecting the wires the other way around will only cause the motor to rotate in the opposite direction. Meanwhile, servo motors have three wires: red, black, and yellow. A servo motor controller comes with pins that are matching these wires so you can just plug it directly.

Attaching Microcontroller to Motor Controllers

Microcontrollers can communicate with motor controller in different ways: 12C, R/C, Serial, or PWM. Be sure to refer to the manual for each microcontroller for specific instructions on proper connection. Regardless of the method you choose, the microcontroller and the logic of the motor controller should share matching ground reference. This can be achieved by attaching the GND pins together. Meanwhile, a logic level shifter is needed if the devices don't share the same logic levels.

Attaching Batteries to a Microcontroller or a Motor Controller

Majority of the motor controllers available today have two screw terminals for the battery labels marked with B- and B+. If the batteries you got are provided with a connector and the controller comes with screw terminals, you could still search for a pairing connector with wires that you can attach to the screw terminal. If this is possible, you need to find another way to link the battery to the motor controller while you can still unplug the battery and link it to a charger. It's possible that not all the electrical and mechanical components you have selected for your robot could operate on a single voltage, and so may need several voltage regulation circuits or batteries.

If you are building a robot with a microcontroller, DC gear motors, and maybe servo motors, it's easy to see how a battery may not be able to power every component directly. Nevertheless, it is best to choose a battery that can directly power as many devices that you need. The battery with the largest capacity must be connected with the drive motors. For instance, if the motors you select are rated a nominal 12 volts, the primary battery must also be 12 volts. So you can use a regulator to energize a 5 volts microcontroller. LiPo and NiMH batteries are the top choices for small to medium robots. Select NiMH if you need cheaper batteries and LiPo if you need light weight batteries. Always take note that batteries are powerful devices that could easily burn your circuits if they are not properly connected. Always make sure that the polarity is correct and that your device could handle all the energy supplied by the battery. If you are not certain, never make assumptions.

Adding Electrical Parts to Frame

You can attach electrical components to your frame through different methods. Make certain that whatever method you use, don't conduct electricity. Usual methods include screws, hex spacers, Velcro, double-sided tape, cable ties, glue, and many more.

Programming Your Robot

Programming is often the last step in building your robot. If you have followed the steps described in the previous chapters, by now you have selected the electrical components such as actuators, microcontrollers, motor controllers, sensors, and more. At this point, you might have already constructed your robots and hopefully it looks something like you want it to be. But without the proper program, your robot is just a cool paperweight.

It requires another book to teach you robotic programming. Instead, this section will guide you on how to get started and what you should learn.

There are several programming languages that you can use to program the microcontroller that will serve as the brain of your robot. The following are the most common programming languages you can choose:

Assembly

This programming language is just a shy away from programming a full-pledged computer, and so it could be difficult to use. This language is ideal to use if you really need to ensure complete instruction-level control of your robot.

Basic

Basic is one of the most common programming languages for robot hobbyists. This is often used in programming microcontrollers mainly for educational robots.

C++

C++ is a very popular programming language. It provides top=level functionality while you are keeping a good low-level control. A variant of C++ is Processing, which includes simplified codes to make the programming easier.

Java

Java is more developed compared to C++ and offers any safety features to the disadvantage of low-level control. Some producers of microcontrollers such as Parallax are making components for specific use with Java.

Python

Python is one of the most popular languages for scripting. It is easy to learn and could be used to quickly and efficiently integrate several programs.

If you have selected a hobbyist type of microcontroller from a known producer, there's a chance that you can find a book that you can read so you can learn how to program in their preferred programming language. But if you instead prefer a microcontroller from a smaller producer, it is crucial to see what language the controller wants to use and what tools are available.

Conclusion

Thank you again for purchasing this book!

I hope this book was able to help you to learn the basic building blocks of robot building.

The next step is to expand your knowledge in robotics, especially learning advanced programming for your robot.

Finally, if you enjoyed this book, please take the time to share your thoughts and post a review on Amazon. It'd be greatly appreciated!

Thank you and good luck!

Book 2
Open Source
By Solis Tech

Understanding Open Source From the Beginning!

Table Of Contents

Introduction

I want to thank you and congratulate you for purchasing the book, *"Open Source: Understanding Open Source From the Beginning!"*

This book contains the basics in understanding the open source concept. What is it all about? Where did it come from? Who creates the open source content? How can software be considered as an 'open source'? What makes it different from the other software that we already have?

These questions are answered in this book. Also included in this book are information relevant to open source, such as examples of licensing, the Four Freedoms of free software use, and ideas about software piracy. This information will help to further understand what it means to have some software that is open sourced.

Real life comparisons are also made in this book in case you become confused or lost in understanding the open source concept. The idea of open source seems very simple, but in reality, it is very complex, with definitions coinciding with the definitions of other concepts such as free software (which will further be discussed in Chapter Two). Listed down in the book are the advantages and disadvantages of open source software, and the reasons why more and more people are becoming enticed with the idea of converting to open source.

If the present generation already dictates the movement of open source software, what will become of it in the future? This question is also answered in the last chapter of this book. Due to the fast-paced advancement of technology, open source will adapt to this advancement with the help of both developers and users.

Thanks again for purchasing this book, I hope you enjoy it!

Chapter 1: The Basics of Open Source

Have you ever wondered how an application you're using works? Every time you use an application and it freezes, do you think about what could have gone wrong? Do you ever think of why applications are constantly updating? These are questions that you would not be asked often. But these questions are very important to you, as a user of the Internet age.

Application programs are comprised of source codes, and these source codes are made by programmers. These codes are what allow you to type words into a word processing document, or to click on that video of cats meowing simultaneously. What you see onscreen are only visual representations of the codes of the program. Your application programs may be paid, or pre-installed in your devices, so you don't have permission to view these codes. Rather, you get the pre-made product, and you as a consumer have no power over it except to use it as instructed.

When you purchase or download an application and place it in your device, it installs a lot of files, but none of these files contain the source code. A software manager is included in your installed files to monitor the application as you use it. Whenever your application gets bugged or freezes, this software manager runs, and it prompts you to file a report to the software's developers to tell them exactly what happened. Once the report is filed, the developers study the bug, fix it, and release an update a few days or weeks later.

But what if you could see these codes for yourself? What if, whenever something goes wrong with the application, you could easily contact the developers or ask for help from other programmers easily? These questions are the foundations of open source, and you are about to learn more about it in the following chapters.

What is Open Source?

Open source is a computer program that has its source code visible to the public. The public – which we can refer to as the users – have the power to view, copy, and modify the source codes to their liking. The source code and the compiled version of the code are distributed freely to the users without fixed fees. Users of open source can pretty much do anything they like with the open source programs that they downloaded, since there are practically no restrictions.

To better understand the concept of open source software, let us use an example of recipes for comparison.

Recipes start off with someone writing them down on a piece of paper. A grandma, perhaps, has a recipe for a cake, which she writes in her recipe book. She passes on this recipe to her children, and tells them that they can use the recipe whenever they like. But, they must make sure to credit her as the original creator of the recipe.

The children recreate the recipe and whenever they are asked where the recipe is from, they would always tell that it's from grandma. One of grandma's children alters the cake recipe by adding strawberries as an extra ingredient. The grandma allows this, given that she is also permitted to use the altered recipe.

This example has the same concept with open source software.

When a programmer writes a code, compiles it into a program, and distributes both the source code and the compiled program to the users, he is giving everyone permission to access everything about the program. Users can run the program, view the code, modify if needed, compile, and redistribute the modified version of the program.

The original programmer, however, would require the users to let him use the modified versions of his program, since it is his to begin with. Aside from this certain restriction, the users of the program have the freedom to do whatever they like to do with it.

Let's go back to the example of the cake recipe. One of grandma's children, the one who added the strawberries, suggests to grandma to add the strawberries to the original recipe. The grandma thinks that this is a good idea therefore she complies and replaces her old recipe with the altered cake recipe.

In open source software, if the programmer is notified of a certain modification of a user, and it is deemed to be a modification that the software needs, then the programmer will revise his program based on that certain modification. This modification is called a patch. The user who has suggested of the modification is now coined as a contributor. This process of adapting user modification to an open source software is called upstreaming, because the modification goes back to the original code.

The concept of open source depends on the communication and collaboration between the software's developers and its users. Bug detection and fixing of open source is made easier because numerous users are working simultaneously to study the source code and to compile a modified, fixed version of the code.

With open source, it is not only the developers who are finding new ways on how the software can be improved and upgraded. The users can also contribute their ideas and knowledge in the upgrading of the software. The original developer or programmer can be called the maintainer who monitors the changes in his or her original software.

Let us then go back to the cake recipe. What if another child of grandma decides to do his own version of the cake recipe? He adds raisins to the cake recipe, and asks grandma if the raisins can be added with the strawberries in the original recipe. Grandma refuses, because she dislikes raisins. Instead of being disheartened, this child decides that he would create his own version of the recipe and share it with the people he knows.

If a certain modification makes no appeal to the developer, the one who suggested the modification may opt to make his own version of the program. This act of not patching a modification from the original program is called forking. A forked program is a certain program that alters the original program in such a way that it becomes its own program.

A forked program can be described as a chip off an old block, since it doesn't necessarily separate itself from the license of the program it originated from, although it may seem like it due to the avoidance of patching. Programmers that collaborate with open source result to forking if their modified versions of the original program are deemed unfit by the program's developer.

Nonprofit organizations are the prime developers of open source software. However, due to the freedom of customization that open source has given both users and developers, even large companies are adhering to the open source culture.

How did Open Source become popular?

During the early times of computing, software followed a protocol and design with everyone conforming to a certain cookie-cutter ideal. Software was yet to be imagined as cost-free, and the developers kept their codes to themselves. But then, during the early 90's, the idea of sharing one's code to the public became an accepted idea to most users. The concept of software being free and open sourced became a reality when, after decades, the likes of Mozilla Firefox and OpenOffice were created.

Open source rose in its ranks when developers started making open source alternatives of commercial software. These alternatives are free and can easily be downloaded from the internet, enticing most users to convert to open source. What made open source rise, however, was the idea of community. Fellow programmers could interact and communicate with each other, and even with the developers, which was unheard of during the early times of computing. People could collaborate with the developers of the software and share their insights.

Open source has also given its users the freedom to fully inspect software before they use it – an action that was impossible to do with closed source software. Users who are into coding try open source and study the code line by line.

The popularity of open source software has been anticipated due to the fact that a lot of people supported the cause. Programmers started creating open source projects to contribute to the cause, and users started to get accustomed to obtaining and downloading open source software. With volunteers signing up left and right, and organizations creating their own programs, the growth and expansion of open source software cannot be stopped anymore.

Chapter 2: History, Comparisons, and Relevance

Open source was not immediately implemented until the early 90's, where more and more people began to realize the importance of being able to share the source code of software without fees and royalties. Like any other idea, open source started out as a small thought of making software free for the public, and grew into the culture that it is today.

The History of Open Source: The Open Source Initiative

Eric Raymond, an American software developer, published an essay (turned book) entitled The Cathedral and the Bazaar in 1997. The essay speaks about two different types of software, which he labels the Cathedral and the Bazaar.

In the essay, Raymond describes the Cathedral to be the type of software in which with each release of software, the source code of the software will be available. However, with each build of the software, the certain code block that has been modified is restricted to only the developers of the software. The examples presented under the Cathedral type of software were GNU Emacs (a type of text editor) and the GNU Compiler Collection (a compiler that caters to different programming languages).

In contrast, the Bazaar is the type of software that has the Internet as the venue for their development, making the code visible to the public. The example presented under the Bazaar type of software was Linux (now a widely known computer operating system), in which Raymond coined the developer Linus Torvalds to be the creator of the Bazaar type of software.

Raymond's article became popular in 1998, getting the attention of major companies and fellow programmers. Netscape was influenced by this article, leading them to release the source codes of their internet suite called Netscape Communicator. The source code of the said internet suit was what gave birth to internet browsers such as Thunderbird and SeaMonkey. Mozilla Firefox, a popular web browser today, was also based from the source codes of Netscape Communicator.

The idea of source codes being free became widespread when Linux was developed, urging people to contribute to the open source cause. Because of the increasing popularity of Linux and similar projects, people who became interested in the cause formed the Open Source Initiative, a group whose advocacy is to tell people about the benefits of open sourcing and why it is needed in the computing world.

Open Source vs. Free Software

Most people confused open source software with free software, as the two terms share somewhat the same advocacy. With understanding, it is not that difficult to tell these two terms apart.

The difference between free software and open source software can be listed down into different points. Although they have their differences, both free software and open source software have a singular goal – to publicize source codes for the users to see.

Free software focuses mainly on the ethical aspect of the advocacy. There are certain freedoms that free software are fighting for when it comes to the use of software, which cannot be given to the users by commercial software. These are the Four Freedoms of software use according to advocates of free software:

•	The freedom to use the software. This means that the user is free to use the software to his or her needs, or as instructed.

•	The freedom to study the source codes of the software. Since the codes are readily available for public viewing, the user has the freedom to view and study the said codes. After he or she reviews the codes, he or she then has the freedom to do the next step.

•	The freedom to modify the source codes of the software to the user's liking. If necessary, the user has the freedom to customize the source code and to create a version of the program fit for the user's specific needs.

•	The freedom to share the modified, compiled source codes to the public. If the program has been modified, the user has the freedom to compile and publish the modified program for the benefit of the other users who may also have the need of the program's modification. The developer of the original program should also be given the freedom and right to use the modified version of the program.

Free software allows its users to do whatever they want with a program. If they want to modify the source code and redistribute the modified code as their own, without the consent of the original developers, then they are free to do so. If the user wishes to use the source code as the base code of a new project that they are working on, then they will not be sued. The ethical reasoning of free software simply states that there are no grave restrictions when it comes to copying, revising, and republishing the already existing software.

Open source, on the other hand, creates programs with the Four Freedoms in mind. The programs which are considered open source are made for the user's convenience and benefit. The common idea of open source is a group of people working on a single open source project, attempting to create a program that will be beneficial to them, as well as the users.

Open Source and Paid Software

Open source software did indeed come from paid software. There are countless of open source alternatives for common, commercially-sold software readily available on the internet. Some examples of this are office suites like LibreOffice and OpenOffice, which are open source alternatives for the much more popular Microsoft Office.

The reason why open source alternatives of paid software exist is mainly the cost. Users would opt to pay less, or none at all, for certain software. Why pay for software when there are free alternatives that can be downloaded from the internet easily? Open source makes it possible for users who cannot afford paid software to experience the basic and intermediate features of the software, without sacrificing the quality of the end product.

Although open source may be the overall solution for users to get a feel of certain software, there are still others who would want to obtain paid software but through illegal means. This is called software piracy, an action that is still evident despite it being illegal in most countries.

Software piracy is the act of downloading or installing a paid software illegally, either through software cracks or illegally burned CDs. The most popular way to obtain pirated software is through downloading Torrent-based software crack, in which the user can get the files through different computers almost discreetly. Since these software are pirated, installing these software requires the user to turn off his or her Internet connection before installing, to avoid being tracked.

Some paid software can be bought once, and shared with different computers or devices. All of the information regarding the sharing of paid software can be found on the software's End User License Agreement or EULA. The EULA is a splash screen shown at the start of the software's installation which contains the contract between the software's developers and the user.

The EULA may allow the user to share one copy of the software to different devices, or it may restrict the user from doing so. Once the user has violated this part of the EULA, it can then be considered as software piracy.

Something that a user should be aware of is a certain license called the GNU General Public License, the license that most open source software adhere to. The license permits the user to copy, modify, and redistribute the modified code, just as long as the source files and the original codes are still documented. This is important in understanding how and why open source software is allowed to move freely across the internet without being coined as software piracy, as compared to paid, propriety software.

With propriety or paid software, the user is buying only the license. He is not allowed to revise the code, to reverse-engineer the code, and to view the code by all means. The only thing that the user is allowed to do when he purchases propriety software is to use a copy of the software that the developer has provided. It may seem like an unfair deal to some people, because a user should be able to own something that he has paid for.

Open source software changes that idea. It gives the user the freedom to see the program's source code, letting the user know the program's 'skeletal system'. Even without paying for the software, the user gets the full potential functions of the software and not just an executable copy of it.

Importance of Open Source

Technology is rapidly changing. Experts are coming up with more ways to improve the lives of other people. It is the same with those who contribute to open source projects. Their advocacy is to create free programs that will benefit the users.

Open source is important in the evolution of quality software. With a lot of people contributing to one singular project, the software that is produced will be the best of its kind as it has been meticulously observed and reviewed by the contributors. Open source gives way for the collaborative effort of different programmers and users, with the users being secondary developers of a certain program. It is an interactive effort, with the users being able to update the program alongside the developers themselves.

The fast paced advancement of technology would often overwhelm content creators to the point that they would stop creating content altogether. Content creators who are left behind by technology's advancement are often working in small groups or on their own, and have no means of help from fellow creators of their kind.

With Open source, this is never the case. Each open source software has its own community to back a fellow programmer up during each build, ready to help out other programmers and users when needed. The open source community's bond with each other is what makes open source catch up with the fast advancement of technology.

Chapter 3: The Benefits and the Downsides of Open Source

The Benefits of Open Source

The most obvious perk of having open source software is the availability of the source code. With the source code available to the general public, people are able to study the code line by line. Students of programming can study the source code and implement some blocks of it into their own projects, honing their skills and improving their code. Users who are meticulous with their software can view the codes and customize the said codes to their liking.

Aside from the source codes being publicized, another perk of having open source software is that it is mostly free, depending on the software's license. Users of open source software do not have to pay a large sum of money to be able to enjoy the full functions of the software. If the license requires the user to pay, the user may still try out the software's full functions before purchasing.

Open source promotes community. If a user encounters a problem with the downloaded software, he or she can seek help from fellow programmers or the developers themselves through a forum. Users and programmers alike can communicate and share their experiences with using the software, helping other users to get used to the software. With other programmers keen on editing and revising the source code, updated and better versions of the software can easily be uploaded and shared within the community for the benefit of the other users.

Also, when something goes wrong with the open source software, the user has the option to fix the problem himself should seeking help be an option that is not convenient for him. In propriety software, this cannot be possible as the license and copyright prohibits its users from ever touching the program's source code.

If the user of propriety software does as much as reverse-engineer the product, then they could be violating the program's copyright and therefore, be taken to jail. Open source software removes this restriction from the users, giving them permission to fix solvable program problems on their own.

The benefits of open source software are not limited to personal use. Companies and businesses are adhering to the open source paradigm due to the endless possibilities at half the price or lesser.

More and more businesses are converting to open source mainly because it is more cost-efficient than purchasing commercial software. Companies also have more freedom with open source software in terms of customization, since they have the power to mold the software to fit their company's needs. These factors are beneficial in the growth and development of businesses in such a way that the businesses need not to put out a large sum of money just to be able to acquire a software that will be utilized in their business.

Open sourcing has become a way for people to have access to the things that they initially did not have access to. Users of software now have the ability to study the source code of the program they are using, and to know how exactly a certain function of the program runs by looking at its specific line of code.

A sense of community is also created between the software's developers and programmers from outside of their firms. Through open sourcing, the developers are able to communicate with other programmers with regards to how the software can be enhanced further.

Some users would say that using open source operating systems grants more security as compared to paid operating systems. For example, if a user installs the Linux operating system, he or she does not need an antivirus or a virus detection software to keep his or her files intact. The operating system itself has security measures for the user. This becomes a benefit for both professional and nonprofessional users because they have more room for important files rather than installing different kinds of applications for protection.

Open source software is made for the people, by the people. It hones itself to the needs and wants of each user. Because of this, there is no need for the user to upgrade his or her hardware every time the software upgrades.

Take Apple's OSX (operating system) for example. Certain updates of the operating system are available to download, with better features than the previous build. However, older versions of the Macbook and the iMac cannot avail of the recent builds as their hardware are not fit enough to accommodate either the size of the downloaded file or the features itself.

With open source software, the upgrades can be coded to fit each user's needs, depending on the user's hardware. If a certain upstreamed version of the open source software is available to download, different downloaders are made available by the developer with the specifications listed beside each downloader, catering to the different specifications of the user. The user himself can opt to customize the code of the program to be compatible with his device.

Allowing the user these freedoms over the software has given open source software a bit of a leverage over paid, propriety software. But then again, there will be nay-sayers who think that open source software isn't the way to go.

The Downsides and Disadvantages of Open Source

Open sourcing has given users lots of benefits, but it is not perfect. Some would still prefer paid software over any open sourced software. Here are some of the reasons why some users do not approve of open source.

If a user is not in any way a technology expert, he or she would want software that is easy to use. Open source software is known to be more technical compared to their paid counterparts. Paid software focuses on its user interface, making the application easy for the user to understand the system. Open source software usually start out with a not so attractive user interface, but with the basic functions of the program intact. As the program gets updated with each build, the user interface changes and adapts to the needs of its users.

Most critics would say that paid or propriety software is still better in a number of factors as compared to open source software. Because more people are accustomed to using paid or propriety software, the idea that there are other types of software available is intimidating to them. People think that open source software is made only for the technology savvy users, with the interface hard for them to manipulate. Why download a complicated software when they can buy a simple, pre-made software that they are already familiar with?

Paid software has become a norm in the everyday lives of users. Large companies such as Microsoft and Apple have made their name known all throughout the world, creating technologies that users and consumers have grown to love. Because of their undying popularity, the rise of open source software is unknown to the general public. And even if they are known, those who are used to seeing the big names are hesitant to try out what open source might be.

Seeking technical help might seem simple with the numerous open source communities readily available, but it may sometimes be inconvenient to the user. Paid software offer professional tech support straight from the manufacturers.

Chapter 4: The Open Source Culture

Open source gives the user freedom to do whatever he or she wants in a software. Who wouldn't want the freedom to edit source codes to their own liking? With open source, this opportunity of customization is available at hand.

Why are more people converting to open source?

With the source code open for public scrutiny, looking for errors will be easier. Other software companies that do not have their source code publicized have their own set of programmers and developers figuring out the bugs in the software. This is an advantage for companies who always require their software to be updated regularly to keep up with the business.

Students who cannot afford the luxury of paid software turn to their open source counterparts to be able to utilize their functions without having to pay a large amount of money. Open source alternatives of Microsoft Office are available for the students to download should they need to use an office suite for their projects.

Some open source versions of paid software are actually better. Paid media players can play certain file types and extensions, but crash once the file extension is unrecognizable. Open source software developers take note of these bugs and create a media player that can play almost all media file types and extensions in high definition. Because of this, even users who are not actually technology savvy would convert to the open source alternatives of paid software just because they've heard and they know that they can get more out of the open source counterpart.

Programmers who want to practice their coding also rely on readily available open source software in their study. Because the codes of open source can easily be viewed and modified, programmers can base their project on open source software and publish it as their own, creating a program fork.

Businesses, on the other hand, turn to open source software for two main factors: cost efficiency and the power of customization. As mentioned in a previous chapter, with open source software readily available to download on the internet, the businesses do not need to spend a lot of money for a software that they cannot customize as their own. Open source gives them the opportunity to keep on upgrading their system as needed, therefore improving the quality of their software with each build.

The flexibility of open source software has enticed businesses to change to open source from propriety software. Businesses would often buy already existing software and attempt to use them as instructed by the developers. Open source software has its own rules and regulations, but if businesses want their software to be something specific, then the developers of open source software will deliver. With propriety software, the business is the one to adjust to the software that they have purchased, an action that is removed once businesses convert to open source.

Examples of Open Source Software

A wide variety of open source software are available for download. These software may be used for utility purposes, for multimedia purposes – anything that the user desires and requires. Here are a few examples of open source software that you as a user have probably heard of.

The prime example of open source software is an operating system called Linux. It is an operating system based off of UNIX that is available to different computer platforms and hardware.

Another example of open source software is the media player called VLC Media Player developed by the VideoLAN Organization. This media player can run a variety of multimedia files at high definition. Its paid counterpart is Microsoft's own Windows Media Player, which before its most recent build can only play a handful of file extensions.

When it comes to operating systems, Android is another popular example of open source software. A company called Android, Inc. (later bought by Google) has developed this mobile operating system using another open source kernel, Linux. It caters mostly to devices which have touchscreen on them, such as touchscreen desktop monitors, tablets, and smartphones, much like its counterpart from Apple called iOS. Android has its own application store called Google Play, where the users can install applications onto their phones mostly for free.

Netbeans, a well-known software developing application, is also an example of an open source software. It is a Java-created application that caters to different programming languages, and can be run on multiple operating systems. Programmers use Netbeans to create object oriented applications using the 24 programming languages that it caters to.

GIMP, or GNU Image Manipulation Program, is an Adobe Photoshop-like application that edits photos and creates graphic images. It has basic photo editing features such as cropping, grayscaling, and resizing, making it a simpler alternative to Photoshop. Like its paid counterpart, users of GIMP can also create animated GIF images, a feature that most multimedia artists are very fond of using.

Video and computer games can also be open sourced. Some open source games such as Tux Racer are available in the Linux package when downloaded. The principle of open source games is the same as any other open source software – the developers merging and collaborating with the users to create quality content to be distributed to the general public. However, the visual quality and elements of open source games are yet to be improved.

Other examples include PHP (a web development language), MySQL (used in databases alongside applications such as Microsoft Access and Microsoft Visual Basic), Python (programming language), Blender (an Autocad Maya-esque application that caters to 3D rendering), and many more.

Chapter 5: The Future of Open Source

What will happen in the future?

The future of open sourcing seems bright. With most businesses converting to open source software and most developers contributing to open source projects, the growth and expansion of open sourcing will continue. Open sourcing gives way for the innovation of modern software technology – with a lot of people working on one simple open source project, there is no doubt that the project will continue to be updated and improved.

Software will only continue to improve as time passes by. Open source software has made it easier for software to improve and upgrade itself due to countless of volunteers who are up to the challenge. While propriety software claim to start software trends, open source software advocates the upgrades of software that will be favorable to the needs of the users rather than to the bank accounts of the developers.

Open source software does not wish to waste the time and money of the user; rather, it aims to maximize both time and money, with the inclusion of effort, of the user when utilizing the software.

Presently, paid software are still dominant over open source software. Paid software have more leverage compared to open source software when it comes to reliability and familiarity, since they have been used by programmers and users alike for decades. There is still a certain percentage of users who are not aware that there are open source versions of their paid software, which they can help improve and customize to their own needs and liking.

More people will be aware of the benefits of open source software in the future. With propriety software releasing more licenses that restrict its users from certain software freedom, the existence of open source will lead to the users converting from propriety software due to the lack of free will.

In the future, there is a possibility that open source will be available not just for software, but also for other forms of content that have sources.

The future of open source as an idea or a paradigm will not be restricted to software alone. With the further advancement of technology, more and more gadgets will be locked down by licenses and warranties which restrict its users from fixing even simple problems that the product may have.

Gadgets are becoming more and more digitized, and copyright restricts people from ever touching or attempting to change the software. Because of this, some people are beginning to open up to the idea of open source not just for software, but also for hardware and gadgets that are used every day.

Let us take tractors for example. Tractors are machines that are essential in farming. If a tractor breaks down, the farmer himself can fix the broken tractor and keep it running again without having to buy a new one. But the modernization of technology leads the manufacturers of tractors to add digital aspects into their products: tractors now have microchips and are operated via computers, therefore are now protected by copyright.

Now, if the new tractor breaks down, the farmer has no permission to fix the tractor himself. He must hire a specialist to fix the problem, or else he goes to jail.

Open source hardware has already started to rise in its ranks alongside open source software. It basically means that users are free to create their gadgets from scratch, using open source hardware. Although the idea seems taboo at present, the fact that gadgets are also being restricted from the users will give way for both open source hardware and software to rise even further, giving users complete freedom over the creation and implementation of the technology that they need.

Content creators are restricted from creating certain things just because of copyright laws. Even artists, who upload videos on websites like YouTube and Vimeo, get flagged just because of a certain song or a certain speech that had some sort of copyright over it. This restricts creative freedom. It also restricts the content creators from creating what they know and love, and sharing it with their viewers.

Will open sourcing become a culture in the future? Surely, with the massive amounts of information available for the users to share freely amongst themselves. Open source software has given way for an idea that will change the world of computing for everyone, and allows everyone to have access to the large chunk of information that was previously not available to them. Transparency when it comes to creating code and building machines will become a fad in the future, as more and more people are willing and able to create content and share it with other users.

Conclusion

Thank you again for purchasing this book!

I hope this book was able to help you to understand better the concept of open source and its benefits to the public.

Finally, if you enjoyed this book, please take the time to share your thoughts and post a review on Amazon. It'd be greatly appreciated!

Thank you and good luck!